KRISTEN EYKEL

YOGA FOR

Transformation

BEYOND ASANA INTO AWARENESS

All rights reserved, including the right to reproduce this book or portions thereof in any form whatsoever, including internet useage without written permission from Big K Productions, except in the case of brief quotations embodied in critical articles or reviews.

Published by Big K Productions
PO Box 8305
Calabasas, CA 91372

Copyright © 2018 by Kristen Eykel

Cover design by Kristen Eykel
Book design by Dr. Samantha Reguieg & Sorrell Schneider
Editing by Mauro Cellore & Wendi Eckstein
Photography by Stephanie Norwood

For information, contact Big K Productions
www.KristenEykel.com

ISBN: 978-0-9843657-6-0

First Big K Productions Printing June 2017
Second Big K Productions Printing January 2018

BIG K is a Registered Trademark

Printed in the USA

Kristen Eykel CHt.

Since her teenage years, Kristen has followed the voice within. It has led her to become a jet-set Supermodel in Paris, TV Host, Kundalini Yogi, Author, Shaman, Reiki Master Teacher, and Certified Hypnotherapist. Combining decades of training, Kristen Eykel is a Spiritual Teacher and engaging Public Speaker who shares powerful insights on how to create a purpose-filled life. A VH1 VJ, she also worked for CNN International, Court TV, E! Entertainment, the Oprah Winfrey Channel, and hosts Mom Ed: Green Living on You Tube. Kristen teaches at the Science and NonDuality Conference, the Sedona Yoga Festival, The Yoga Expo LA among other events. She has appeared on the cover and in the pages of numerous publications worldwide, such as *Yoga Journal, Health, Fit Pregnancy, The Chicago Tribune*, plus radio, TV & online interviews for her unique expertise.

In 2014, she founded Sacred Circle Teachings - a physical & spiritual Yoga, Hypnosis & Reiki training academy designed to empower the teachers of tomorrow with the sacred knowledge of all time. Her devoted and loyal following fill her yearlong Mentorship program, *Awesomeness Training*, and assist Kristen's personal mission to unite the world in joyous Soul awareness and conscious evolution for all.

She is the proud mother of two home birthed kids who inspire her with the true meaning of Yoga - trust and strength, honesty and balance, her daily aspiration and inspiration. Find out more at www.KristenEykel.com.

"Kristen has created a symphony of beautiful tools which are perfect for this time in the world. While I consider Kristen a dear friend of mine, I can vouch for her being a friend to you as well. Authentic and Supportive. I highly recommend Kristen's work.
~ Karena Virginia ~ Spiritual Teacher, Healer and author of "Essential Kundalini Yoga"

*"More addictive than a Vicoden (in a good way)…..If you are just a neurotic mess, the soothing incantations of this model beautiful instruc*tor *with 20 years experience in Shamanism, Reiki and Kundalini could calm even the suicidal."*
-LA Weekly "BEST of LA"

Introduction

*"It takes 40 days to break a habit;
90 days to gain the new habit;
120 days and you are the habit;
1,000 days you are Master of it."*
—Yogi Bhajan

What has stopped you from having the life of your dreams so far? Do you think that you not good enough? Do you think you need to know more? Do you procrastinate or make yourself so busy that you don't have time to follow your dreams? How do you access YOU when life and work and family pull you in different directions?
Do you want to change all that?

I will show you how.

My journey with yoga began in 1990 when I was a young super-star model in Paris feeling torn apart mentally, physically and spiritually by the life. After years of perfection at the cost of starvation, and world travel combined with exhaustion, it took an anxiety attack in the London tube for me to make a change. Yoga became the way for me to learn to live IN my body, rather than treat it as my commodity. Listening to my inner spirit began my journey into healing and self awareness. I trained with teachers from the South Pacific to South America, became a Certified Hypnotherapist and a Reiki Master Teacher. This combination became my daily Yoga, a healing practice that I share with my students everyday, and share with you here now.

Most people think of yoga as an exercise routine that you do on a mat as a way to get more limber or reduce stress. Yoga is actually a 5,000 year old science and it is not just what you do in a sweaty class, it is how you learn to live your life. Awareness can never come by comparison with another, or by inflating your ego to be more "spiritual" than someone else. It comes by being honest to your soul.

You see, when you keep repeating certain thoughts, you literally create yourself everyday from these habitual mental patterns over and over again that you have grown accustomed to believing are YOURS, even if they are something that you adotped from somewhere or someone else. Over time, this energetic habit weakens your ability to hold new thoughts or awareness. It literally becomes a spiral of negativity, like an addiction that is challenging to break on your own. This cycle of negativity governs every subsequent choice - the actions you take, the words you say, the activities you participate in - from the most minor to the most expensive. Unwittingly, some of these myriad choices have cost you dearly in life. You may have lost out on opportunities in work, or love and family harmony, social connection, or even physical health.

Overtime these habits of thinking can deteriorate to the point of deep imbalance that can be toxic and difficult to remedy. And the amazing thing is? You probably never even saw it coming.

Yoga for Transformation is specifically designed as a 6-week program that opens new self awareness, and that guides you to remember that **you** are the common denominator of every circumstance in your life. You are the only one who has actually lived your life, and you are the only one who has made these choices of your own free will, even if you were unconscious of them at the time. You discover that you are either repeating habits of low vibrational thoughts and beliefs about yourself that have limited your power, *or not*. The wonderful discovery is that you feel truly free, maybe for the first time, to align your actions with awareness, your thoughts with knowing, and empower transformation today.

Goal and Purpose of this Planner

Are you ready to learn the truth about Yoga?

Yoga asana, or the physical postures you may have practiced in class, are the embodiment of certain concepts that are meant to serve as examples of how to live a balanced life. It is meant to usher in *Enlightenment*, literally the embodiment of more light. that you can use to see more clearly. In other words, if you are in a balance pose, learn to understand where the balance is in your life? The union in Yoga is that of the self with the Higher Self, of a structural integrity that ushers in a sense of peace and mental alertness that we know of as Awareness.

What if you could shift your awareness just enough to be able to see this way too? And then shift even more to begin to experience this? And then transform completely and begin to live this way? Your life and everything and everyone in it would become transformed by this awareness.

Yoga for Transformation is a unique combination of mental, vibratory, auditory and physical connections that you will make in this system that will break your habitual tendencies to sell yourself short or make excuses for why you can't. You will expand your awareness of who you are already born to be, not just who you defaulted into.

This transformation will help you to literally recreate how you view yourself. By completing this program as a wonderful result, you will learn that the world you want to experience is already within you, or you could not be feeling its pull. You will learn to honor the feelings of your body, seperate from the thinkings of your mind.

First alleviate the feelings that you are not enough, so that you can then infuse your being with a new sense of empowerment.

Make space for Awareness to land.

This course teaches you the ability to formulate a new identification, and this becomes the key to achieving your heart's desire. Learn who you are, discover what you truly want, so that then you can move towards achieving it, because you cannot achieve that which you desire if it is waging an unconscious war within you.

To do this, you first need to learn about your stumbling blocks and methods of self-sabotage. This program will show you where you want to stop and where you are frankly, lazy. Where do you make excuses with yourself or make bargains with others that do not serve your goals?

In *Yoga for Transformation*, you learn to hold yourself accountable to these tendencies, and develop the stamina and discipline required to motivate yourself beyond them. You will discover what really matters to you and what you have a passion or calling for that makes your time in this life meaningful.

Armed with this knowledge, you can then apply these tools of introspection and insight across all aspects of your life, benefiting your family, career, social group, your education goals and so forth, making it easier than ever before to create a plan of action that stems from your heart. More importantly, you'll learn how to better follow it through to see it manifested in your life.

Yoga for Transformation helps you learn to not only understand yourself, but to create a true love and respect for yourself. This honest respect for self is what allows you to build the roadmap to your truest heart's desires, to deeply have insight of your strengths and weaknesses, and discover how to best align this awareness to support your goals.

Self-reflection is almost impossible to achieve on our own. We need our mentors, gurus and community to assist us in holding up the mirror so that we can see where we shine and where we have room to grow. This course is given as a way to finally be able to hold this new reflection for yourself, help you gain an enlightened self awareness, and confidently create a life that matters to you and to the community who loves you.

How to Use this Journal

Every day for the next 6 weeks, you will be presented both with an *Affirmation for the Day* to journal from, and a physical action, or *Technique for the Day* to undertake. This process should take you no more than one hour each day to explore and experience, but your commitment to the process should be total. It is the constant connection to the thought and its practice that will more deeply elicit the change and new being that you wish to experience. The *Affirmation for the Day* has a few prompts for clarity, to help you get your connection to the meaning of this new statement of Being. Feel free to write, in your own words on the blank page, what this Affirmation, combined with the Technique lends to your understanding of how it may apply in your life.

Read the *Affirmation for the Day*, and then on the page next to it, write out how this thought lives within you. How can this thought become part of your life or understanding about yourself? Do you even know what it feels like to hold this thought? Is it something that you already understand or is it a challenge to grapple with? Let yourself journal freely to this point and then allow this *Affirmation for the Day* to come up in your conscious mind often throughout your daily activities. See how many different ways you might apply this same thought to different challenges.

Following the *Technique for the Day*, let yourself discover how you feel when you combine this thought with this action. Is it easy and intuitive, or do you struggle to hold onto its meaning? The challenge will then be how you will incorporate each daily lesson into your everyday experiences, not just in isolation as you study them. For example, on Day 12 when you are presented with the *Affirmation for the Day* about Patience, you will be required to exercise this quality - maybe by standing in line or by waiting on hold during a phone call.

Do this journaling and practice every day *without skipping a single day* for maximum results! Part of what determines our success or failure is also the ability to stick to a plan without deviating into the thickets of apathy, boredom, or frustration.

At the end of 6 weeks, you will absolutely discover a deeper understanding of yourself, what moves you to action and what prevents it. Quite likely, it will be something that you may not have even expected! You will also discover your connection to your desired

outcomes, and learn how this connection helps you on your path as it currently exists, or how you wish for your current path to alter to more clearly drive what matters most to you.

As well, you will be building a Vision Board, so start collecting your images and words now. On Day 10 it will start to be made and it will be revisited or adjusted often in the following weeks. Don't know what a Vision Board is? Check out the necessary tools and description on pages 8 & 9.

There will be scheduled checkpoints along this journey to allow you time to reflect and adjust your continuation on your chosen path. Every 7th day, there will be a mini check-in on how you are feeling in this process. Here you will examine what you have discovered about yourself that is in your way, and also what strengths or realizations support your journey. The recognition every 7 days will also amplify your progress as you make your way to completion on Day 42.

The Week 3 checkup is the halfway point. You will re-examine how you are coming along with your goals as a whole, and your feeling about them now from your practice to date. This moment also gives your the freedom to evolve your initial goal. Are you still true to that initial feeling or has it morphed into something new?

After 42 days, you will have incorporated this new way of living - a new habit - into your life, so that by the end of the 6th week, you are solid in your goals and in your feelings of how you are creating them everyday. You will now know how your everyday actions and thoughts align, conflict or mesh with your goals, bringing them into manifestation.

The steps entail:
- Your Vision Board as one of the tools to help you to "see" it
- Journal writing and affirmations that will help you to language it
- Mudra, postures and physical techniques that will help you to embody it

Everyday work in this manner will help you to truly feel yourself change in real time. Things will change or grow from week to week to week. Your daily practice will put everything into motion, so that at end of this process, you will put all of the pieces together and write an essay about your transformation. What have you discovered, learned, and experienced, and how have you grown or altered your perceptions?

Set Your Intention

Set yourself up for what you think your intention is now, knowing that it may change, and inviting that it may need to change. At the outset, imagine the biggest goal you can possibly create. Have it feel beautiful, and as vibrant and rich as you can possibly imagine. As you go through this process, invite yourself to step up to *who you would have to be* in order for this beautiful manifestation to exist - beyond it being a fantasy - to experience it as becoming a reality.

This is a different perspective than what you may have held before. It is a relevant one however. Who do you need to grow up and become in order to have what you most want to experience come to fruition? This contemplation requires grit, focus, determination, and patience to stay the course out of love for yourself and passion for what you are creating. This process of evolution helps you to override the petty fears that prevented you from getting it before now. You will uncover places where you have been stuck, and reservoirs of strength that are your gift. You will discover that you already are the person - perfectly positioned - to manifest your dreams.

You may not know how to get there yet. That is perfectly ok. If you already knew how to get there, you would already be there! Allowing yourself to discover the way through is the true joy of being present in your process. Being present also allows us to examine what we are carrying that is in the way for our fabulous new energy to land.

Consider this perspective:
- We all seek to cultivate new things, for example stuff that represents status or achievement. But without a driveway or some safe place in front of your house, where are you going to park the expensive, new vehicle if it were delivered?
- If you love to entertain and wish to have an elegant dinner party with flowers and table settings, yet your table is covered with piled up laundry, bills, and junk, then you must clear and clean the chaos so that you have the space to invite your guests to enjoy your magnificent feast.

- You so profoundly want to invite love into your life, but you are filled with bitterness and resentment, fear and jealousy. Love requires patience and kindness to flower. You need to weed the garden of your bitterness and resentment first to allow a blossoming of the feeling of love to take root within your own heart before you can discover the feeling of love for another.
- Watching him work, an observer asked Michaelangelo how he created his gorgeous and life-like David out of cold block of marble.

"That's easy," the genius replied, "I just take away anything that's not David."

Where are you required to take away everything that is NOT your intended outcome in order to discover the masterpiece waiting to be revealed?

This new place to grow from, this clearing, requires new ideas, feelings, and situations. The truth that you will discover, is that they all start within US! If we are toxic or overloaded with junk, muddled and unclear, there is no room for anything beautiful, new or vibrant to land and flourish. We must clear our own being in order to not only realize what we want, but to have space within us for it to manifest.

As a human with a body and mind of our own, we are required to become stewards of our own energy in order to make this contribution to our world. Our world does not rush to fill us. We expand to encompass what we need to fill it with. We can choose love or fear, sadness or triumph, joy or resentment. We choose by every thought, deed and action what we are made of.

In this endeavor for the next 6 weeks, you have an opportunity to see what you are already made of and how to cultivate the next steps for who you are becoming. The path to your enlightneed awareness is already within you. Now let's clear away the junk so you can find it.

Happy journaling and we can't wait to applaud your discoveries!

Vision Board

A Vision Board is a literal roadmap of our desires and dreams that are beyond language. Your conscious mind is what is reading these words right now and deciding to follow through with the instructions or not. However, your subconscious mind has been whispering to you that *this is such a great way to manifest what we want!*

Our subconscious mind is our center of feeling and of dreams. It is represented by the Right Brain. It is emotional and fluid and not always "rational". Indeed the rational part of our being, demonstrated in the Left hemisphere of the brain, is the place of analysis and sequencing. Both are necessary components for self-understanding and reflection, so we seek to entrain both of these parts of your awareness in Yoga for Transformation.

Begin to collect pictures and words that inspire you from magazines or the Internet. Put them into an actual and/or virtual folder to keep until it is time to build your board. You may not use all of them, so collect as many as you like, even more than you need. Allow them to be concepts or images that strengthen you, that remind you of your goal, or of your feeling about what inspires this goal within you. Color, texture, and shape are also part of this language for the mind and internal awareness to utilize, so be playful with these dimensions of perception as well.

Leave space on your vision board for more things to come in, or for you to adjust the collection as the weeks progress. Allow yourself to use the Technique for the Day to assist in the creation and evolution of your Vision Board. Perhaps, come to the Board creation *after* you have practiced your Daily Techniques or perhaps at the time of day where you feel the most relaxed and connected to your inner peacefulness or creativity.

You will need:
- Large poster board
- Magazines (the greater the variety, the better)
- Scissors
- Glue sticks or double stick tape
- Any color pens or pencils, markers or other decorative writing items

You can be as inventive as you wish. This is YOUR expression! Some folks like it clean and orderly, others like to add objects like feathers or ribbon. The point is your personal self expression that will imbue this lifeless board into a magic vision of what inspires you. You will be posting this board somewhere in your environment that you can see and reflect upon everyday. Allow it to be beautiful and make you feel happy. That is all that matters. You will build this on Day 10, so start collecting now and add to it every day. Keep your eyes open for anything that inspires you!

Week 1 - Day 1

Set your Intention

Begin by setting your intention. It can involve anything and be either modest or grand. For example:

- I want to get married.
- I want more love in my life.
- I want to complete my degree.
- I want to be successful in business.
- I desire vibrant health.
- I want to be of service to my community.

For the moment, just pick one that you will be focusing on. Write this down with great clarity and detail. You will eventually create it as one sentence, but for the moment, write a short paragraph to yourself that outlines the feelings and desires that this desire contains. WHY this matters to you is more important than HOW this will manifest. For the moment, don't worry about the HOW. Simply allow yourself to experience why this experience is important and what it means to you in any way that you currently understand it. State your intention clearly and with as much feeling as you can express. Allow yourself to ruminate upon this for the entire day today, and feel how it would feel if this desire were to manifest in exactly this way.

Week 1 - Day 2

Technique for the Day

Mountain Pose

Become as solid and as rooted as a mountain. Stand upright with your feet a couple of inches apart and your back tall and straight. Imagine that there is a cord at the top of your head lifting your head to the sky. Feel your body as it hangs to the Earth from this cord. Feel your feet as if they have roots growing into the soil. Use this to root and ground yourself and feel what it feels like to be in your body at this moment. Let your arms be long and straight at your sides, palms facing forward as if you had beams of light coming from them to light your way forward. Keep active energy in your arms, but they are not overly tense. Feel yourself as immovable as a mountain, as solid as a stone. Set a timer and do this for two minutes in the morning, then frequently throughout the day. You can do it at the bus stop, on the train, waiting in the grocery line, at work, in every situation of the day. See how you can feel yourself being solid and present in every situation, no matter who you are with or where you may be. Play with this feeling of groundedness and strength as if you grew from the Earth. Repeat the Affirmation for the Day in your mind as you experience the Technique.

Affirmation for the Day

I am present.

Today I am fully present in my life. I experience the clarity of this present moment right now. Instead of being scattered, being present gives me access to a higher state of being and awareness. I enjoy *this* moment for myself. I can see and experience the richness of my being here now. There is always something to be grateful for and aware of in the moment. I no longer rush through moments. Instead, I see what is around me clearly and truly enjoy the awareness that this brings. I enjoy myself within this moment of presence.

Week 1 - Day 3

Technique for the Day

Diaphragmatic Breath

Sitting comfortably, close your eyes, and begin to follow your breath. Place your hands on your stomach just under your rib cage and feel yourself inhale completely.

Emphasize this feeling of deep breathing by allowing your stomach to expand fully and have it push your hands away from your body. As you slowly exhale, feel your belly draw all the way inwards, releasing the old, waste air from the bottom of your lungs, so that you have room for more air on the next inhale. This pulling in and pushing out by your diaphragm, will allow you to deeply expand your lungs, rib cage and lower back and will offer an increase in the breadth of your inhales and exhales. Start with a count of 4 as you inhale and a 4 count as you exhale. As you breathe, focus on your diaphragm expanding with the inhale, drawing the belly inwards on the exhale. Feel the sensation of gathering more oxygen into your bloodstream as your awareness increases. Keep this awareness and relax into the breath. After a few moments, allow your breath to extend to a count of 6 in and 6 out. Allow yourself to relax further, and discover if you can extend your count to 10 in and 10 out. Set a timer and enjoy 5 minutes for breathing as you focus on the Affirmation for the Day.

Affirmation for the Day

I am my breath.

Breath is the one thing I cannot live without. It is primary. We hold our breath when we are feeling things - fear, anticipation, and anxiety. When I breathe fully through it, the anxiety subsides. When I breathe, I have power. Instead of holding my breath and waiting, I take deep breaths and know that holding my breath prevents me from feeling. It is only by breathing fully into the process that I expand myself into the experience, being, and action required by this moment. When faced with a challenge, I give myself a moment to connect with my breath before I respond.

Week 1 - Day 4

Technique for the Day

Pranam Mudra

Sit in a comfortable position. Bring your hands together at your heart center in prayer position. Palms are flat to one another, fingers straight upwards, thumbs resting on your sternum. Close your eyes as you press your palms together. Feel all of the parts of your hands touching. Feel this engagement with about 5 pounds of pressure between your hands. Your shoulders open, keeping your neck long and spine straight, become aware of the point in the center of your chest between the thumbs and your spine. Imagine that you are opening up a doorway here in your center and imagine the 2 halves of your brain and body in balance and in harmony. See it, sense it, feel it, and experience it as balanced. Breathe from your diaphragm as you concentrate on the Affirmation of the Day. Set a timer for 5 minutes.

Affirmation for the Day

I am my center.

I sense or feel that I am my own strength, my own port in the storm, my own center. Rather than looking outside of myself for someone to fix or save me, I now know how to calm and center myself and find my grounding. I am my own center. The thing outside of me is not my center. It is here, within me now.

Week 1 - Day 5

Technique for the Day

Combine the three techniques from Day 2, 3 and 4. Stand in Mountain pose, with palms in Pranam Mudra and breathe from your diaphragm for 5 minutes. Focus on the Affirmation for the Day in the center of your being.

Affirmation for the Day

I am present and centered with my breath.

My alignment allows me to be present in every situation, without judgment and fear. I exist in a neutral and receptive place. It is normal that things might be distracting, so I notice that when I drift into judgment or negative self speak, I then smile at myself, and let the distractions pass. I remember that this is me growing in my self awareness, so that I can return to my breath and center. The mechanism of my understanding, is not just in the presence of my breath and center, but also in the awareness when I have strayed from my chosen path. My conscious choice to be present, breathing, and centered now open up possibilities that I had previously not seen, acknowledged, or recognized.

Week 1 - Day 6

Technique for the Day

Rock Pose

Come to the floor kneeling with your legs folded underneath you, and sit on your heels, which are together pressed inro your buttocks. Use as many pillows as needed under your hips or ankles if you are unused to sitting in this fashion and if this is more comfortable. Elongate through the spine by lifting up through the crown of the head. Relax your hands on your thighs. Set a timer and see if you can surrender here for five minutes. If your legs become uncomfortable, briefly stretch them out and then come back to the Technique. Your body will gradually adjust as you practice this posture. Connect to the Affirmation for the Day as you connect to the Earth.

Affirmation for the Day

I am connected to the Earth.

Grounding to the Earth causes me to feel more solid. I can relax into the gravity and power of Mother Earth and feel strength and balance pour into me. Whenever I am "in my head", I can find support and strength, by releasing my awareness down into the core of Gaia. This is the place of stability that is always present and available for my use, no matter where I am.

Week 1 - Day 7

Review

Reflect back upon this past week and the challenges, discoveries, and realizations that you have made. Write them down. No matter how small or insignificant they may seem. Allowing yourself to recognize them as they come up is important. As you think about this week, whatever comes to mind is your answer. Write it all down and utilize the Techniques and Affirmations from this week to inform your insights.

Week 2 - Day 8

Technique for the Day

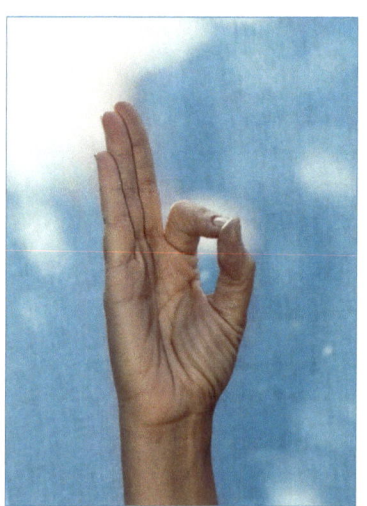

Gyan Mudra

Seated comfortably, connect the tips of the thumb and the index fingers together on the same hand, making a circle of them. Keep the other three fingers extended. You may do this mudra simultaneously on both hands. Place the palms face down towards the Earth on your lap or knees. This is grounding and roots you to the Earth. This mudra brings peace, calm, and stability. Hold this Mudra for 5 minutes as you feel the Affirmation for the Day working within you.

Affirmation for the Day

I am grounded.

I am stable. I am calm and balanced. My well being depends upon me being in my place of strength. I allow myself to feel this connection now and invite this feeling into my daily practice. I call upon the sense of being Grounded in times of imbalance and stress. I feel instantly calmer when I am Grounded.

Week 2 - Day 9

Technique for the Day

Sit in Rock Pose with your hands on your legs in Gyan Mudra facing down towards the Earth. Hold this position for 5 minutes while you feel what the Affirmation for the Day offers.

Affirmation for the Day

I am Earth.

I reflect and experience myself as a living component of Mother Earth. My molecules are made of this Earth and all of my physical needs are supplied by it. Air, food, water and every physical object I experience is from this planet's bounty. I am one part of the many parts of Earth.

Week 2 - Day 10

Vision Board

Today you build your Vision Board. Gather up the ideas and feelings, words, color and moods that you have been collecting in your folder for the past 10 days. Maybe add some new ones from today. Give yourself as much time as you need. You will continue adding to it over the next few weeks, and will revisit this process at Day 21, so don't worry if it is not complete. Allow it to unfold.

Begin with any of the Techniques or Affirmations of the Day which have inspired you so far, and take a few minutes to connect to your Intention as you originally intended it on Day 1. After you feel centered and inspired, begin to play!

Glue your images and words to the poster board. Feel free to flow with your design. Perhaps cluster certain concepts together in quadrants of the board, or create a story with the images. Decorate this as beautifully as you can. Perhaps you listen to music that you love in the background. Create the scenario for YOUR greatest connection to Joy and Well Being. Use this as the launch pad for your desires to manifest, so that every time you pass by your board, you feel inspired by its message.

Week 2 - Day 11

Technique for the Day

Alternate Nostril Breathing

From sitting in a comfortable position either in a chair or on the floor, lengthen the spine upwards and downwards simultaneously. Feel your tailbone reaching into the earth as the top of your head lifts to the Infinite as if suspended by a string. You may wish to sit on the edge of a pillow or blanket to assist this posture if you are unaccustomed to sitting straight for any length of time.

Gently close your eyes and bring your right hand up to cup your nostrils. The right thumb will be resting near the right nostril, the left ring finger and pinky by the left nostril. Close the left side & inhale through the right nostril to a slow count of 4 to start with. At the top of this breath, close the right nostril, retaining the breath for a slow count of 4. Open the left nostril, exhale out of this side on the same 4 count, and then inhale on the left to a 4 count, closing the left nostril, and retaining the breath for a count of 4 before opening the right nostril and exhaling through this side. Inhale through the right side and repeat the cycle. When you can, gently increase the count to a 6 or 8 count- only going as high as you comfortably can.

Set a timer for 5 minutes while you reflect upon the Affirmation for the Day. With practice, you can work up to 10 minutes or more for maximum benefit. Your capacity will improve with practice.

Awareness - *During pregnancy, breath holding is not to be practiced at all. Instead, follow the alternate nostril breathing pattern, but eliminate the suspended breath.*

Affirmation for the Day

I am balanced.

When I breathe in this manner, my brain and emotions, thinking and feeling centers are harmonized. I find balance in the hemispheres of my brain and in the sides of my life. I find balance in my diet. I am balanced in my relationships.

Week 2 - Day 12

Technique for the Day

Shuni Mudra

Touch the tip of the second finger to the tip of the thumb lightly. Hold it firm enough so that you can feel the pulse of energy between these two tips, yet not so hard that your fingers turn white. You can do this with both hands. Rest them face up on your lap and close your eyes as you hold the affirmation for the day in your mind. Practice this mudra for 5 minutes now while you reflect upon Patience, then throughout the day as a way to bring Patience into every situation.

Affirmation for the Day

I am patient.

Allowing myself to understand my patience is a true gift. When I need to work on patience, the world around me gives many ways to practice. Standing in line, comforting a sick child, speaking to an angry person, my demands at work- all are opportunities to cultivate the calm and focus of Patience. This is my gift to offer myself and to those around me.

Week 2 - Day 13

Technique for the Day

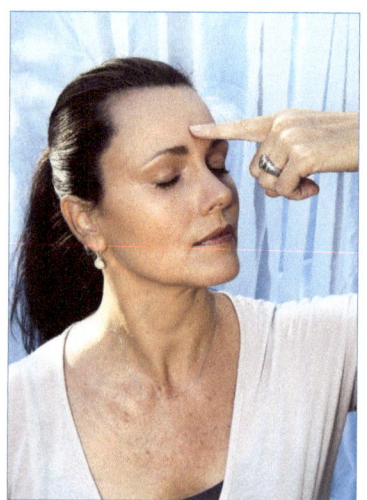

Sitting in a relaxed position with your eyes rolled upwards and inwards, connect to the Pituitary Gland. You will feel a slight pressure in the muscles of your eyes that indicate your connection to this Master Gland. It feels like you are crossing your eyes backwards into the center of your brain. This gland regulates your hormone balance and is a valuable tool to shift your awareness of any situation to one of more presence and calm. Know that you will forget to hold this alignment and will frequently need to re-establish the rolled up and inwards feeling throughout the 5 minutes of practice time. Relax with your hands in your lap.

Mentally repeat the Affirmation for the Day while connecting with the Pituitary Gland to feel the positive effects.

Affirmation for the Day

I know.

Connecting to my intuition allows for a deeper sense of understanding. Knowing occurs when I still myself to allow the thoughts that are under the surface to rise to my consciousness. I know what I want. I know how I feel and I know what is important to me. I feel how it feels to KNOW.

Week 2 - Day 14

Review

1. Reflect back upon this past week and the challenges and discoveries that you have made. Write them down. No matter how small or insignificant they may seem, allowing yourself to recognize them as they come up is important. As you think about this week, whatever comes to mind is your answer. Write it all down and practice the Techniques and Affirmations from this week to inform your insights.

2. After you have practiced your Techniques and Affirmations, take a moment to sit quietly and focus your mind upon your intention. What matters to you and how do you feel about it today.? Then, take some time to collect more images, words and feeling items for your Vision Board. Add them to your folder. You will be working on the Vision Board again on Day 21. Continue to keep your eyes open in the upcoming weeks for items that interest you or feel appropriate to your desired outcome.

Week 3 - Day 15

Technique for the Day

Seated Rocking Posture

From seated in a chair or on the floor in a gentle cross-legged position, hold onto your knees and roll your eyes upwards and inwards as you inhale from the diaphragm and rock forward through the spine. Lift the sternum and reach the chin long in front of you, dropping your shoulders back and down. You will feel a stretch run down the spine to the tailbone. As you exhale, sink back, curling the spine into a c-shape and drawing the chin towards your chest. Continue to roll through the spine, lifting forward on the inhale, and curling back on the exhale. Set your timer for 3-5 minutes and enjoy the feeling of this movement opening up the channels of the spine, your mind, and organs. Repeat the Affirmation of the Day as you continue this Technique.

Affirmation for the Day

My intuition is clear and strong.

I practice feeling the strength of understanding on a visceral level and it empowers me in my choices today. My intuition serves me in feeling my way through situations that are beyond intellect or thinking. My intuition is clear and focused and is always working in my best interests.

By allowing myself to take time to listen within, I discover how clear and strong my knowing is. I feel/ sense/ see/ know more than ever before. I allow myself to be guided by this knowledge from within.

Week 3 - Day 16

Technique for the Day

 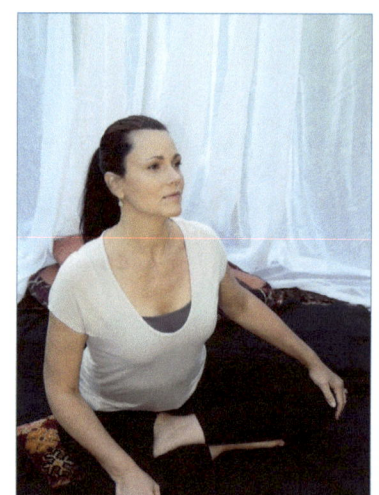

Seated Circles - both directions

From seated upon a chair or the floor in a lightly cross legged posture, begin to roll the body forward from the diaphragm as you inhale in a circular fashion, exhale as you roll back through each hip. Let the movement be initiated from the center of your body at the naval point as you go around, rather than moving from your shoulders. You will feel this stretch in the lumbar and throughout the organs and hips. This should feel deep but relaxing. After 2.5 minutes in one direction, reverse the legs if they are crossed, and go in the opposite direction. Flow with the feeling of being in your Instinctive nature and let your internal knowing be stimulated by the movements.

Affirmation for the Day

I am instinctive.

I follow my gut instincts. I cultivate opportunities to ask my own advice. My instant knowing is important to heed, so I pay attention and follow this guidance. Today, I practice my knowing of simple things - what to eat, what to wear, who to spend time with. These simple actions allow me to more confidently address deeper knowings as they arise.

Week 3 - Day 17

Technique for the Day

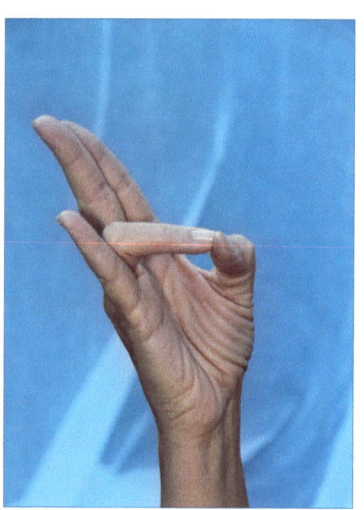

Ravi Mudra

Touch the tip of the ring (third) finger and the tip of thumb together firmly but gently on both hands. The other three fingers are straight up. You can rest your hands palm up on your lap. Do this mudra while seated comfortably for 5 minutes. Connect to the Affirmation for the Day while you feel the gentle pulse between the fingertips.

Affirmation for the Day

I am strong.

I feel how to support myself as I get stronger. I am more capable and resilient than I ever previously knew. I feel this now as I go about my day. I practice my strength by my capacity to overcome obstacles to my wellbeing and my belief in myself grows. I feel strong in my communication, in my body and in my heart.

Week 3 - Day 18

Technique for the Day

Breath of Fire

Seated comfortably, focus on strongly exhaling through the nose. Every exhale draws the diaphragm deeply towards the spine. Close the eyes and roll them upwards and inwards to connect to the Pituitary Gland. Allow the inhale to naturally occur through the nose and soften in the belly. Completely focus on the exhale only and get into a rhythm you can comfortably maintain. This IS a challenging breath, and it may make you feel hot. It is supposed to! Align yourself with your inner knowing and feel confident that you are more than capable of this practice. Create the sensation of Freedom in your body and mind as you practice. Start with 2 minutes initially, but work up to 5 minutes or longer.

Awareness - *During pregnancy, Breath of Fire is not to be practiced at all. Instead, follow the breath with long, deep inhales and exhales. If you feel faint, simply inhale deeply and relax. However, by focusing on a strong exhale and flowing into a comfortable pace, you should feel more of a workout in the belly than faintness in your head.*

Affirmation for the Day

I am free.

My sense of freedom is within me. I am free to choose what I will say and how I will feel. My freedom is neither given to me nor withheld from me by anyone. I feel the feeling of freedom in my ability to eloquently express myself, my thoughts, and my truth. My feelings are free to be experienced and I freely share of myself with others.

Week 3 - Day 19

Technique for the Day

Savasana - Corpse Pose

Sitting on the Earth or firm surface, place blanket or pillow underneath your knees. Gently roll down onto your back and lengthen the spine away from your hips as you elongate towards the earth. Once completely down, allow your feet to gently roll outwards, relaxing the entire leg towards the outside edge of your body. This will gently open up the hips and release through the lumbar. Shoulders are back and down. Lengthen through the neck away from your ears. Rest your arms at your sides, gently opened with the palms turned towards the sky in a receiving gesture. Set your timer for 5 minutes and let your thoughts melt into the Affirmation for the Day. Feel how expanding feels in this Technique for the Day.

Affirmation for the Day

I am expanding.

As I expand in my capacity to understand and learn about myself, I notice how much bigger my life becomes. I allow the confining ideas and thoughts of my past to ease away now, making room for new, larger thought forms that I am expanding into with pleasure. I expand into the world around me and feel relaxed, balanced and supported.

Week 3 - Day 20

Technique for the Day

Hakini Mudra

Sitting easily, bring the hands up in front of your chest. Gently touch all tips of the five fingers on each hand to the tips of the opposite hand's fingers. Allow the palms to move away from one another as far as they comfortably can while keeping the fingertips together. Rest them here. On each inhale through the nose, touch the tip of your tongue to the roof of your mouth, and on each exhale, allow the tongue to relax down again. Follow this pattern for 5 minutes as you hold the Affirmation for the Day of Focus.

Affirmation for the Day

I am focused.

The more I focus my attention, the greater clarity of thought I hold. The more I focus, the more I am able to accomplish. My day and thoughts become clearer than ever before and I notice how much more productive I feel when I simply focus on the task at hand. I enjoy the feeling that focus affords me.

Week 3 - Day 21

Reflection

This is your halfway mark in the program. Congratulations for sticking to it and for keeping yourself accountable to what you most desire! At this marking point, examine your vision board and what you have started. Revisit your initial intention and now, using the tools of reflection that you have gained, go into this vision and beginning destination as you outlined three weeks ago. How does it feel to you now? Do you have new insights or desires? Have you let go of aspects within yourself that have altered this course to a slightly, or even radically new heading? Allow yourself to be fluid and gracious with yourself, while still maintaining strength in your convictions and owning what truly drives your passion and enthusiasm for living a life well made. Using your new insights, rewrite or alter your initial vision or goal. Keep the language succinct and to one sentence. Rework your Vision Board as needed to reflect other aspects of your desired outcome that are more feeling based than language based.

1. Reflect back upon this past week and the challenges and discoveries that you have made. Write them down. No matter how small or insignificant they may seem, allowing yourself to recognize them as they come up is important. As you think about this week, whatever comes to mind is your answer. Write it all down and practice the Techniques and Affirmations from this week to inform your insights.

2. Revisit your initial intention as you had written it on Day 1. Does it still ring true? Has it shifted or evolved to allow another aspect to become present? Rewrite your goal with the new understanding you have gained, or sharpen the language of your goal to be more concise.

3. Revisit your Vision Board. Look at it with fresh eyes and see if it still reflects what you feel about where you want to go. If not, add to, layer or remove images and words that need to be updated, and create the next level of your goal as reflected by the understandings that you have gained in the past 3 weeks.

Week 4 - Day 22

Technique for the Day

Ball of Light Meditation

Comfortably seated, begin to rub your hands together rapidly. Close your eyes and focus on the sensations in your hands. After about 60 seconds, gently open them, allowing them to be slightly curved and facing one another at your heart level. Create a Ball of Light in the cupped palms at heart level. Feel the tingle or the warmth, the glow or the sensation of what this energy ball feels like. Begin to imagine the feelings and ideas about what you most wish for yourself, your community or family. Pour all of your desires here until the ball is full and rich. Maybe it has even expanded, so allow your hands to part wider if necessary. Take as long as you need to really feel the connection to the energy in your hands as well as to the feelings created by the ideas in your mind. Once it is full, keeping your eyes closed, raise this ball high above your head and imagine that you are placing it into your 8th Chakra. This chakra is many feet above your head and is represented by a huge, sparking white ball of light. Allow yourself to give this ball of your intentions to the Divine. Imagine that you can see it absorbed into the bigger light. Return your hands to your sides and feel the peacefulness that this offering to your

Affirmation for the Day

I am enough.

I discover that I am enough to manifest whatever I want or need within myself. I need no one's permission to feel myself. I choose to feel how being Enough is a marker of my growth and wisdom. Feeling Enough is a birthright for every human to embrace. I fully embrace the sense of what feeling like Enough means to me. I share this feeling of Enough with the world around me.

Week 4 - Day 23

Technique for the Day

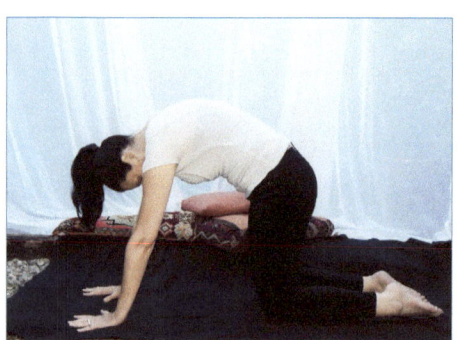 

Cat / Cow

From kneeling on the floor, place your hands to the floor directly under your shoulders, with the knees hip width apart. Feel evenly balanced in your body on your hands and knees. As you exhale, tuck the tailbone down towards the Earth and your chin towards your chest. Feel yourself pressing your heart up towards the back of your spine, and arch like a Cat. As you inhale, draw the chin forward, elongating through the spine and lifting the tailbone to the sky. Be aware of feeling the lift through the front of the body, stretching your body upwards from the belly, rather than compressing in the lumbar. Arms remain straight and shoulders stay down, away from the ears. Set a timer for several minutes and allow your body to flow with the Affirmation of the Day in your mind.

Affirmation for the Day

I am flowing with my life.

The feeling of flowing is what allows me to meet challenges that may arise. I feel and experience a softness within myself that is my strength. Too rigid, I will break. I must flow and bend gently to allow new energy and awareness to flow within me. As I do so, I feel emotions and thoughts rise up to my awareness that give me access and insight into who I am at my deepest levels.

Week 4 - Day 24

Technique for the Day

Varada Mudra

This hand gesture is made with the left hand and symbolizes the giving of gifts or blessings towards that which is before you. From standing or sitting, the left arm hangs naturally down towards the earth, all five fingers close and the palm facing actively forward. The right hand is extended upwards, elbow bent close to the side of the body, fingers close together. Feel that the right hand is extending a blessing forward to your path, as if you were taking an oath. Hold this awareness of bestowing Generosity before you and give it to yourself as a promise. Practice this mudra throughout your day, as often as you can. Sense how each time you do it, you connect consciously to the act of blessing yourself and others.

Affirmation for the Day

I am generous.

Generosity within my being allows me to feel generous with others around me. As I gift myself with this blessing, I am surrounded with the feeling that Generosity bestows upon me and everyone around me equally. I feel nourished and effortless in the giving of this gift. I feel rewarded by my intention to hold generosity within my being.

Week 4 - Day 25

Technique for the Day

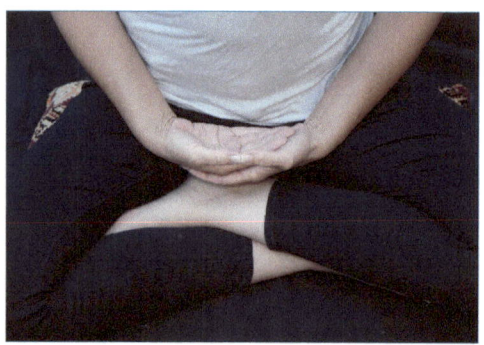

Buddha Mudra

From sitting upright, hands at the level of the navel, allow the right palm to rest cupped in the left for women, left cupped in the right for men. The tips of the thumbs touch to complete the feeling of contemplation. Palms are relaxed and there is a gentle pulse between the tips of the thumbs into the hands. Close your eyes and roll them upwards and inwards to the Pituitary Gland. The Affirmation for the Day rises and falls with your breath as you sit quietly within. Set a timer for 5 minutes, and allow yourself to come to this posture frequently throughout the day to reflect on what this feeling generates within you.

Affirmation for the Day

I am thoughtful.

Thoughtfulness is a practice. I allow myself to hear and understand my own thoughts as a way to better understand myself and my motivations. I am thoughtful with the words I choose to think and speak, and am thoughtful in the actions that I take as a result. Thoughtfulness is reflectd in the world around me and I notice the difference in how I receive the gifts from others around me that stem from their acts of thoughtfulness.

Week 4 - Day 26

Technique for the Day

Practice 5 acts of kindness.

1. Give and/ or receive a sincere compliment graciously.

2. Share your time and thoughts generously.

3. Offer and receive assistance effortlessly.

4. Listen attentively to those addressing you by looking them in the eye.

5. Look into your own eyes in a mirror and say how grateful you are to your body for its support of you in your life.

Affirmation for the Day

I am kind.

Being kind to the world begins by being kind to myself. Kindness is a blessing in my life, and I feel it flowing through me. I receive kindness as a gift from others and I share this feeling effortlessly with the world around me. As I practice kindness for Self and others, I grow stronger in my own sense of wellbeing and awareness of how important being Kind truly is.

Week 4 - Day 27

Technique for the Day

Place your right hand on your heart chakra in the center of your chest. Place your left hand on top. Close your eyes and roll them upwards and inwards, as you meditate on the feeling of Sincerity. Set a timer for 5 minutes and enjoy the feeling of your heart center expanding and how you can grow its capacity for sincerity throughout your being like a halo of light. Notice how you feel. Is this experience a challenge or is it already a present experince within you? Become aware of how Sincere you actually are with yourself.

Affirmation for the Day

I am sincere.

Sincerity is a cornerstone of my being. It is a feeling of ownership of myself and my word. I speak with sincerity so that I may express my truth easily. Giving the weight of sincerity to my thoughts and actions allow me to grow in my capacity of sensing sincerity in others. Sincerity is my bond and promise to be honest with myself. Sincerity grounds me in my truth.

Week 4 - Day 28
Review

1. Reflect back upon this past 4 weeks and re-read in your journal the thoughts and inspirations, understandings and awareness you have discovered. Write it all down and practice the Techniques and Affirmations from this week to inform your insights. Notice which Affirmations were easy to hold onto and which were challenging. Notice which Techniques you enjoyed and what they made you think about or feel as you practiced them.

2. Revisit your goal as you have it currently. Does it still ring true? Has it shifted or evolved to allow another aspect to become present? Rewrite your goal with the new understanding you have gained, or sharpen the language of your goal to be more concise.

3. Revisit your Vision Board. Look at it with fresh eyes and see if it still reflects where you want to go. If not, add to, layer or remove images and words that need to be updated. Create the next level of your intentions as reflected by the understandings you have gained in the past 4 weeks.

4. Begin to pay attention to how your Techniques and Affirmations for the Day are living with you. Are some coming up in your consciousness over and over again? Are some lessons being reflected in them? Conversely, are some of them irritating or bothering you? Take a deeper investigation into your feelings and experiences, and begin to discover what it is that you are responding to. Often when we go deeper into our process, we begin to hit "walls" or places of resistance that need greater care and awareness to overcome. Notice what kind of walls you may have been hitting and how you normally would cope in these situations in the past. Do these coping mechanisms still serve you? Or, are you now understanding how they may need to evolve as YOU are evolving? Be completely honest with yourself. Use the Techniques and Affirmations that you enjoy the most to overcome your resistances. Focus more intently on the ones that seem more challenging. Have patience with yourself as you uncover WHY it is so uncomfortable for you. Often times, this answer is the gift waiting to be uncovered for your progress.

Week 5 - Day 29

Technique for the Day

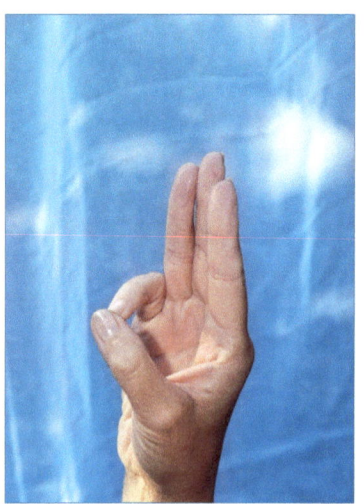

Buddhi Mudra

Firmly touch the nail of little finger with the tip of the thumb and push the little finger down towards the palm. The other three fingers remain straight up and together. for clear and intuitive communication. This mudra can be done with one or both hands. Hold it firmly, but not so strongly that there is uncomfortability. You can rest your hands palms up on your lap, or hold them in the air in front of you with your fingers at shoulder height, elbows bent to your sides.

Affirmation for the Day

I honor my word.

My word is important to me and to others. What I say and how I mean it, matters. If I give my word, it is my bond and I follow through. I give thought and intention before I give my word. I stand by my word. I use language carefully and precisely to mean what I feel. I say what I mean. When I misspeak, I immediately address it and make the appropriate corrections. I notice that the power of my word changes the world around me in a positive and important ways. My word creates how the world and relationships interact with me, both positively and negatively. Therefore, I am aware of the impact of my word so that my word speaks for me.

Week 5 - Day 30

Technique for the Day

Ego Eradicator

From sitting cross legged on the floor, extend the arms up and out to a 60 degree angle straight from your shoulders. Fingers are curled into the palms, with the thumbs extended towards each other above the head, pulled away from the palm. Close your eyes and focus on the area of energy above your head between your hands. Begin Breath of Fire for 1-3 minutes. As you finish, inhale deeply and then holding the breath, bring the thumb tips to touch above your head. Exhale as you open the fingers wide and pull up in the body from the base of your tailbone, imagining all of this energy moving UP to the tips of your fingers. Hold the breath out for a moment, then inhale as you sweep your arms down through your energy field to rest in prayer position at your heart. Rest quietly as you notice the feeling in your body and mind.

Affirmation for the Day

I am truthful.

The sense of being Truthful is important to me. It regulates the types of relationships I engage in, the way I speak about myself and helps me to feel connected to my goals. My truth is my power in a fundamental way. I live according to this truth, and I feel freedom to decide who I am based upon the sense of "walking my talk". I live up to the truth of who I am.

Week 5 - Day 31

Technique for the Day

Standing Forward Fold

Start by standing with your feet hip width apart (4-6 inches) with your weight evenly between them. Both feet face forward. Place your hands on your hips at the crease of the hip flexor in front of your body and lift your upper body from the ribcage away from the lower body, creating a sense of elongation in the spine. Hinge at the hips with your chin lengthened forwards and your shoulders down your back. Your neck and upper body should feel pulled away from your lower body. Keep this sense of length as you fold as far forward as you can, keeping your knees straight, but not locked. Prevent your back from arching in the middle. Once you are as far over as you can go, run your hands up the back of your legs to lift these muscles away from the floor, pulling them around your hips forward to lift your tailbone even higher. This should help you to feel a deeper hamstring stretch and melt a little deeper in the spine. Relax the head and neck down towards your toes and fold your arms across one another to increase the feeling of dripping from the hips to the Earth. Rock your weight forwards and backwards slightly to find neutral position between heels and toes. Now relax your thighs. Hang down in this manner for at least 1 minute and try to come into this posture often throughout your day. Notice how you feel an increase of blood flow to your head and heart. To come up, bend the knees a small amount and curl upwards as you inhale back to standing.

Affirmation for the Day

I am aware.

Awareness flows through me and my senses. I am aware of my body in the space around me. I am aware of how textures feel and flavors taste. I bring awareness to everyday situations with a new sense of clarity that helps me to find new understanding in things I thought I previously understood. My awareness gives me different insights and greater perceptions into my feelings and motivations.

Week 5 - Day 32

Technique for the Day

Sitting in a chair with your feet to the floor or cross legged in Easy Pose on the floor, begin to repeat the mantra, "Sa, Ta, Na, Ma" as your touch each tip of your fingers to the thumb - one sound per finger. Eyes are rolled up to imagine that the sound's energy pours in through the top of the head, and into the middle of your brain. It exits out through the 3rd Eye like an "L" shape. This mantra means, "Birth, Life, Death, Rebirth" and is a powerful mantra and meditation for the brain's healthy functioning.

"Sa" press the index finger or Jupiter finger, with the thumb tip.
"Ta" press the middle finger or Saturn finger, with the thumb tip.
"Na" press the ring finger or Sun finger, with the thumb tip.
"Ma" press the little finger or Mercury finger, with the thumb tip.

Set a timer for 11 minutes and follow the pattern of 2 minutes outloud. 2 minutes in an audible whisper. 3 minutes chant silently, but keep the fingers moving, connected to the 'L' pathway in the head, and keep the tongue moving. 2 minutes in an audible whisper. 2 minutes outloud to end. At the end of 11 minutes, inhale deeply and raise your arms up in the air. Strongly shake your arms and hands. Your whole body and spine can move. Exhale. This shaking is an important way to finish the meditation, as it flows the energy into the whole body. Relax for a few minutes and feel the sounds absorb into you before you go back to your day.

NOTE- As you do this meditation, you may see or feel things moving through your mind. This is actually excellent and is part of what you are releasing. Don't hold on to any of it. Simply allow it to flow away in the mantra.

Affirmation for the Day

I am intelligent.

My intelligence is a gift that I give to myself and share with the world around me. My intelligence increases as I seek to learn and to understand. I have innate intelligence specific to me, and I hone and honor this gift.

Week 5 - Day 33

Technique for the Day

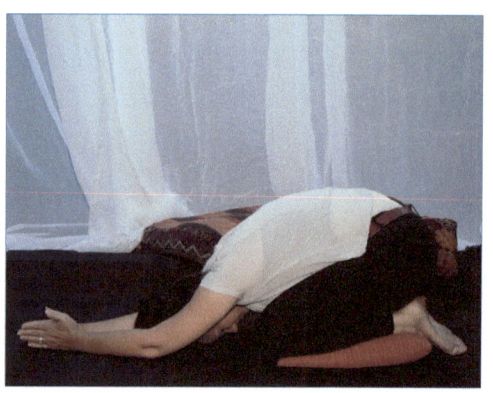

Guru Pranam

From sitting on the floor on your knees, rest your buttocks to your heels. Have your knees a few inches apart to your comfort level. If your thighs or hips are especially tight, you may put a block or pillow under your tailbone for support. If you like, you may also rest your shins on a pillow with your toes over the end to offer support for your ankles. Inhale sitting tall and lift your hands high so that you create length down your spine. Exhale, and bring your forehead and arms to rest on the floor in front of you. Put gentle pressure on the center of your forehead as it rests on the floor and draw your awareness up to this point. Arms are extended in front of you with the palms pressed together in prayer pose, left thumb locked over right for women, right locked over left for men. Keep your awareness on the Affirmation of the Day as you go within. Try to hold this pose and relax here for up to 5 minutes. Come back to this posture throughout your day to bring grounding and clarity to your mind whenever you feel upset or stressed.

Affirmation for the Day

I am perceptive.

My perceptions drive my understanding of the world around me. How I perceive my world creates feelings within me. I choose to perceive with greater delicacy and detail so that I may have more insight into myself and view my world with greater clarity. I pick up on details that I might otherwise have missed, and my powers of perception open doors into situations and my relationships in new ways. I use my new powers of perception with great enthusiasm, as this allows me to find and notice more opportunities that I might previously have missed.

Week 5 - Day 34

Technique for the Day

Heart Breath

Start by sitting comfortably with your eyes closed. As you inhale, draw the breath down into your lungs filling your diaphragm into your waist and lower back. Feel yourself rejuvenating your body with this intention. As you exhale, imagine that there is an opening for exhalation in the center of your sternum, right at the breast bone. Every exhale, feel yourself releasing tension and stress, anxiety or unhappiness through this opening. Inhale filling with love and joy, exhale sadness and fears. Continue to allow the opening in the chest to expand, and perhaps feel as if water or wind is pouring out of this opening, carrying your emotions back to the Earth for clearing and grounding. Give yourself completely over to this experience. Feel any emotions or review any images that come up and let them all be poured away to the Earth. Set a timer for at least 5 minutes to allow yourself to relax into this experience. Practice this many times throughout your day, or even with your eyes open in the moment of a stressful encounter with others. Exhale all of the feelings from your body so that you may feel a shift in the tensions within and around you.

Affirmation for the Day

I am loving.

I am connected to the love in my heart and to the love given to me by others.

I experience love in many forms. For myself, intimate family members and for strangers around me, love loves through me and flows into the world. I make space for love in my own life to enter more freely and I share its resonance with all effortlessly around me.

I enjoy the feeling of love in my body, mind and heart. Love is a gift that is shared with me and others equally and as I experience it, I sense, feel and hold more of it within me.

I find that all is a reflection of Love.

Week 5 - Day 35

Reflection

1. Reflect back upon this past week and re-read in your journal the thoughts and inspirations, understandings and awarenesses you have discovered to date. Write it all down and practice the Techniques and Affirmations from this week to inform your insights. Notice which Affirmations were easy to hold onto and which were challenging. Notice which Techniques you enjoyed and what they made you think or feel about as you practiced them.

2. Take a moment to sit quietly and imagine or visualize your intentions. See its outcome exactly the way that you wish for it to occur. Feel how you would feel if it were to unfold in exactly this way. Notice any anxiety around this. If there is a tickle of a fear or hesitation, use your Techniques and Affirmations that you have practiced that you enjoyed most to apply them to clear these emotions. Do this until you can hold a clear representation of your vision in its perfect, completed form in your mind.

3. Revisit your Vision Board from this perspective. Add images and words that inspire you based upon the feelings that your imagination of attaining your goal has shown you today. Have you discovered something new? Have you let go of or added a new dimension that is now of greater relevance? Keep working with the idea of being receptive to new understandings and awareness to flow through you as you evolve, open and grow. Allow your goals to reflect this opening and growth.

Week 6 - Day 36

Technique for the Day

Heart Breath in Guru Pranam

Come to Guru Pranam as on Day 33. From this posture, begin to practice the Heart Breath from Day 34. Set a timer for at least 5 minutes as you allow the posture and the breath to clear away any fears or concerns. Feel them flowing back down into the Earth as you allow the rejuvenating breath to fill your body as you inhale. Concentrate on your Affirmation for the Day in this position.

Affirmation for the Day

I am forgiving.

I feel a sense of forgiveness for myself. My past mistakes have been what allow me to learn about myself today. By forgiving my past, I feel freedom to create my future. My sense of forgiveness allows me to have greater patience and understanding for the world around me. I feel forgiving towards myself and others. My relationships improve with the gift of forgiveness that flows from my heart.

Week 6 - Day 37

Technique for the Day

Stand in front of the mirror and really look at yourself in your eyes. Examine the physical characteristics that make up who you are - distinct and individual from anyone else. Notice things you may have previously dismissed as imperfections in a new light. See how these individualize you from anyone else. See how they add to who you are. Look at this person and speak aloud the Affirmation for the Day directly into your own eyes. Feel how it feels to claim yourself as Beautiful. If it makes you uncomfortable, seek to discover why. If you feel silly, ask yourself why speaking to yourself makes you self-conscious? In fact, realize that you speak to yourself all the time, usually in less than flattering speech. Changing the attitude and owning yourself as a beautiful being is more challenging than you might think. So stick with it for 5 minutes at a time and keep at it throughout the day until you begin to feel that you indeed, ARE beautiful - inside and out. Feel that you can claim yourself, and then feel that you are worth the claims you make for yourself.

Affirmation for the Day

I am beautiful.

My beauty is unique and personal. I claim myself as beautiful - in my speech, in my actions and in my thoughts. Owning myself as beautiful inside and out, allows me to own others' beauty in the world around me. My sense of beauty is my own and I share myself beautifully with the world around me.

Week 6 - Day 38

Technique for the Day

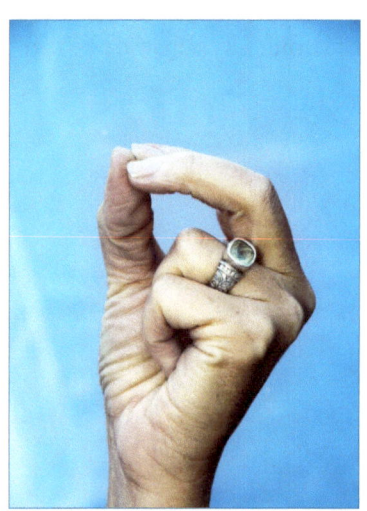

Kubera Mudra

Press the tips of the thumb, index (or Jupiter Finger) and middle (or Saturn Finger) together tightly. The ring (or Sun Finger), and little (or Mercury fingers) are bent and rest in the middle of the hand. You can hold this mudra with either or both hands. This mudra focuses your energy to help manifest your goals and desires. Set a timer for five minutes to hold the mudra while you practice the Affirmation for the Day in your mind. Use this technique throughout the day to help you to make decisions and to focus upon your desired goals.

Affirmation for the Day

I am bountiful.

Feeling Bountiful is an expression of my well-being. I give generously to others because I feel the sensation of richness and fulfillment. I live in a bountiful world. There is ample opportunity for me to express myself in my life in a way that feels generous.

Week 6 - Day 39

Technique for the Day

Dance

Put on music that inspires joyous movement from your body. Put on headphones if need be, but have the music comfortably loud enough so that your thoughts disappear into the rhythm and sounds. Let yourself move in any way that is organic to you. Abandon yourself to this feeling of joyousness in your body's movements. Let yourself feel the happiness that comes from the vigorous expression of your body's freedom to express itself in dance. Feel the bliss run throughout your system from the top of your head to the tips of your toes. Let yourself completely go - unapologetically and with great delight! Repeat the Affirmation for the Day as you dance and perhaps even sing it out as you move. Let yourself fly with the feeling of whatever Bliss means to you!

Affirmation for the Day

I am bliss.

Bliss is a state of being that is my birthright. I feel bliss when I care for my body and care for my loved ones. I feel bliss in the simple pleasures of being alive. I experience bliss in numerous ways. Bliss inspires joy and happiness within me. I share the sensations of bliss with my family and community that there may be more bliss felt in the world around me.

When I am in bliss, everything feels right with my world.

Week 6 - Day 40

Technique for the Day

Ujjayi Breath with So Hung Mantra

To do the breath, sit comfortably in a chair or on the floor. Begin to allow the breath to come in as long, gentle inhales through the nose and release with long gentle exhales through the nose. Keep the breaths the same length. As your breath evens out, begin to feel a slight constriction in the back of the throat as you inhale and exhale. The breath should now sound more like the ocean or almost as if you were to whisper. Connect to this sound and let your throat and rhythm become relaxed. Now, add the mental mantra of So Hung. As you inhale think SO, and as you exhale with the slight constriction sound, think HUNG. *So Hung* means "I am Thou", and connects you to the source of your being. See if you can continue for up to 5 minutes, letting yourself flow into the feeling of being one with all that is.

Affirmation for the Day

I am.

I am anything that I say that I am. My word matters, my thoughts have meaning and my actions follow the course of the beliefs that I hold for myself. I am whomever and whatever I say that I am. I am a part of everything, and everything is a part of me. I am all that there is. I am here. I exist. I AM.

Week 6 - Day 41

Technique for the Day

Garuda Mudra

Interlock your thumbs together as you place your hands with splayed fingers over your heart center. Men have the right hand on the chest with the left on top, women hold the left closest to the chest with the right hand on top. Hold the fingers open wide across the chest, fingers up towards the collarbones, as if you are warming your heart center. Hold this position for up to five minutes as you recite to yourself the Affirmation for the Day. Feel that you are imbuing yourself with this energy of protection, safety and security.

Affirmation for the Day

I am bountiful, blissful and beautiful. Bountiful, blissful and beautiful I am.

I am all of these wonderful things and so much more. I hold myself as precious and protect myself from any harm, both from myself and from my actions. I keep myself pure and harmonized with the light that I am. I recognize and honor myself and seek to hold myself in the Light of Love in everything that I do. I am valuable and I hold myself as precious.

Week 6 - Day 42

Completion Day

Congratulations! You have completed a 40 day cycle of investigation, insight and discovery.

- Allow yourself to examine your past six weeks of practice and experiences. Notice ways you may have grown through altered perceptions or shifted awareness within yourself. Notice how you may see more of your own patterns being reflected in the world around you, offering you insights and clarity on a level that is deeper than ever before, perhaps even in ways that you never anticipated.

- Allow these understandings and feelings to infuse you as you turn your thoughts towards your Vision Board. Examine it from a feeling perspective. Does it make you feel inspired by looking at it? Do you feel excited by the possibility that your vision inspires? Take another moment to spend time reviewing this roadmap to your desires. Change, alter or realign anything that strikes you as less than harmonious.

- On a fresh page, write your intention and awarenesses from a new position of power. Affirm that this is what serves your highest greatest good and feel that this is already yours. Experience within yourself the shifts that have allowed you to gain a new perspective and ownership of your life.

- Take a moment to reflect on what was the most powerful aspect of this journey and what you had to invite in as well as let go of to make it possible.

- Write a 200-300 word essay that pulls everything together from the past 6 weeks of practice and discovery. Use this as an oppurtunity to solidify your understanding of what you have gained and how you have grown.

- Honor yourself for the work you have done for yourself, for never giving up and for completion of your task.

- Continue to practice the Techniques for the Day and the Affirmations for the Day and allow yourself to utilize this process for any goal that you set your mind to.

Remember, you are who you say you are. You are absolutely capable of creating any experience for yourself that you choose. Aim as high as you desire, and flow from your heart. On behalf of your friends, family and loved ones, I too thank you for your service to us all!

May the Longtime Sun shine upon you
All Love surround you
And the pure Light within You
Guide your way on.

Many blessings and sat nam-

Kristen Eykel

Reflections

Reflections

www.ingramcontent.com/pod-product-compliance
Lightning Source LLC
Chambersburg PA
CBHW042032150426
43200CB00002B/21